ALSO BY ROSE KLIX

Fifty Years of Poetry 1962-2012

Pastiche of Poetry, Volume I, Poems titled A-M

Pastiche of Poetry, Volume II, Poems titled N-Z

Religiously Inspired Poems

God, My Greatest Love

Fiction

My Short and Long-Stemmed Stories

Nonfiction

Petals and Thorns of This Lifetime

Eat, Diet, Repeat

Rose Klix

EAT, DIET, REPEAT
Rose Klix

Published June 2013
ISBN-13: 978-1484915783
ISBN-10: 148491578X
Library of Congress Control Number:
2013909154

Cover Design: Kimberly McCarron Anderson
Interior Design: Rose Klix with assistance from
Shell Media, Johnson City, TN
http://www.ShellMediaonline.com

Author information at
http://www.RoseKlix.com

DEDICATION

Thank you, Rob, for loving my spirit –
no matter my physical size.

PREFACE

This collection of poetry explores all aspects of my much repeated life process of eating and dieting. I experienced choices and temptations with both my internal twins, Cassie and Polly. Let me explain:

Greek mythology named the Gemini male twins Castor and Pollux. I was born under the Gemini sign and always feel I am of at least two minds. I blame my internal female Gemini personalities, who I name Cassie and Polly.

Sassy Cassie wants to socialize and eat and eat and eat. She doesn't just chew with one sweet tooth; all hers are sweet. Cassie must be pushed to exercise. She loves to practice sedentary tasks: reading, writing, playing piano, watching movies and TV. As a result, when I allowed this twin to control, we topped out at 205 pounds. We wanted to party, but Polly is such a drag.

On the other hand, Prim Polly studies food charts, plans her diet, and frowns when offered sweets. She appreciates exercise. The Wii Fit Plus sports package, DVDs for Yoga, Zumba, and Tai Chi provide a variety of actions. With Rob's help, Polly and I drag Cassie to walk at least thirty minutes on most days.

Cassie's viewpoint seeps into poems which talk about sweets. I try to keep Polly from lecturing too much about good diet practices, but her voice is in those poems which may sound preachy.

Polly says, "Choose wisely, and chew sufficiently."

Cassie says, "Enjoy an occasional treat before the expiration date."

I had fun relaying my experiences with food, diet, and exercise. With much effort, I achieved my goal to weigh less than Rob. Maintenance is my continual plan. I hope you enjoy a long, healthy life.

Note: Any offered advice is based on personal experiences. Consult your health care provider before applying any tips to your lifestyle.

TABLE OF CONTENTS

INFLUENCES

FAMILIES

Families are wonderful.
Families are great.
Families sit you down
to clean your plate.

They tell you to eat all that —
all your peas and lots of cake.
Then confess you might be
getting just a bit too fat.

MY MODELS

Odd-sized ladies from my youth,
Momma Cass and Twiggy,
each influenced me whether
to fast or become a big-y.

Now Rob's the hero I imitate.
His size is what I long to be.
My husband is slender and strong.
My goal: to weigh less than he.

JUST A SLIVER
OF STOLEN CRUMBS

Momma top shelves her Heath candy bars.
Daddy smokes Winstons.
Jim buys Lays chips
from his paper route money.

I salivate thinking about
German Chocolate cake
in our dented loaf pan.
A long skinny slice won't be noticed.

Crumbs drop from sticky fingers.
Momma's coming.
I gobble faster than taste buds enjoy.
Cellophane tears but stretches enough.

I wash evidence from my hands.
Momma opens the frig.
She eyes me, feels my guilt.
Liquid is missing from her 7-up bottles.

"I didn't do it, Momma."
She doesn't believe me.
Jim savored my punishment,
and her pop – I'm sure.

I'm never satisfied
with leftovers.
I want more.
I always want more.

FUN FOOD THOUGHT

For a lifetime of enjoyment,
I suggest eating your way
through to the end.

Mom said, "Try everything
three times before you
determine if you like it."

First time,
it may not be
fixed properly.

Second time,
because it requires
an acquired taste.

If after the third time,
you pucker your lips
and shake your head,
definitely you don't like it.

I'm not yet sure I like pizza.
There are so many kinds:
thin crust, thick crust,
meat lovers, veggie lovers,
with anchovies or without,
Sicilian, Italian, Chicago-style.
I must try any and all combinations
at least three times before I decide.

If I don't keep good records,
I may have to start all over again.

SQUEET AND TWIRLY

Mother's quilt shop kept her
super busy: sewing, teaching and
selling cloth she loved.
The hours flew past so fast.

She hungered for more minutes
with her hobby, turned career —
time once shoved aside for
active home and family.

Dad retired to yard work.
Often he worked as her unpaid chauffeur.
Most days, at noon Dad called "Squeet."
When translated his line meant, "Let's go eat."

Mom, involved deep, often replied, "Twirly."
Not surprising, her reply, meant "Too early."
One clerk, who heard this exchange daily,
nicknamed Dad *Squeet* and Mom *Twirly*.

RECIPE FOR SUCCESS

My recipe for success:
don't expect too much
and be grateful for what I receive.

Dad told me many times,
 "It's not what you want, but
what you get that makes you fat."

I notice I must have received quite a bit,
because I just totaled my tallow storage.
Now I want less adipose abundance.

BORN OVERWEIGHT

Never skinny –
from the beginning,
fat gathered as I feasted.

I learned my habitual
good nutrition avoidance
from seasoned experts.
My parents enjoyed
sweets, starches,
empty calories, and
their long-enough lives.

No excuses now.
My personal health survives
in my adult hands.
My food – my mouth –
my responsibility.

TEXTS WITH MY INTERNAL GEMINI TWINS

Cassie: hungry

Polly: just 8

Cassie: celery not 'nuf

Me: carrot?

Cassie: NO! real hungry

Polly: dieting?

Cassie: nope

Me: we r

Cassie: not me

Polly: have 2

Cassie: sugar?

Polly: shut up!

Me: stop

Cassie: fries?

Me: tempting

Cassie: HUNGRY!

Me: me 2

Cassie: scream bar?

Polly: no!

Me: ok

Cassie: 2 to 1! Yay 4 ice cream!

Polly: won't make goal

Me: nxt wk

LETTER TO MOM

Mom, I miss your
New Year's Day
Open House celebrations.
Christmas was over, but
the new calendar started with

visits from family, neighbors,
friends, coworkers and
church acquaintances;
all gathered to pay
attention to you
on center stage.

You planned for weeks,
sent out invitations,
wondered what time
who would show up,
worried no one would attend.

I was enlisted to help
make hard candies,
fudge, varieties of cookies,
cakes, and brownies.

You taught me to set a pretty table.
I created fans of silver forks and
spoons you purchased with
Betty Crocker coupons.

I spread the napkins
in whirling patterns.
Candle centerpieces sat in
homemade pine wreaths.
To smiling guests, we served
treats on glass plates with space
for punch or hot coffee cups.

We planned all month,
prepared all week.
The successful event
took hours before and during.
Clean-up lasted the evening.

I learned hostess skills
and polite conversation.
It's difficult to face the new year
without you and your party, Mom.

I AM FROM

I am from:
the Four Roses,
Chrysler New Yorker,
Stanley Home products,
Columbus Street explorations,
Rapid City, South Dakota,
strawberry patch fenced from birds.
mandolin strumming,
singing unlimited verses of Alfalfa Hay,
player piano and homemade pickles,
miniature western towns,
sewing for necessity and quilting for art,
"finer than frog hair,"
"beans, beans the musical fruit,"
white glove pouring tea from
silver pots after church service,
English, German and Dutch ancestors,
corn fritters and creamed eggs on toast,
poor become middle class
high school dropouts to first college graduate.

HABITUAL HABITAT

Coffee break,
smoke break,
snack break –
work place
works against
my efforts.

If I do not indulge,
I do not break.
I force myself to walk
around the building,
stretch, then frown at co-workers
who forget to return to work.

DON'T MATCH

Compatible crunchy
peanut butter and smooth
sweet jelly worked well
together for decades.

We don't match
or color coordinate.
I am not the same as you.
You are not me.

Chocolate birthday cake
smothered in vanilla ice cream
didn't compromise their
separate flavors.

Stop pointing out differences.
Diverse ideas resolve problems.
Celebrate our combined
good tastes and individuality.

We're both unsatisfied,
but full of ideas and plans.
Lay out your smorgasbord
with thoughtful samples.

I'm hungry for change.
Wait! Talk. Listen.
Don't jump into the blender.
The solution isn't a smoothie.

EVALUATION

CALORIE COLLECTION

Calories collect,
but not on my cupboard shelf
or out of sight in the frig.
My stash isn't in my purse,
but sits visible to the world:
on my waist, my thighs,
under my arms and chin.
I'm saving, but forgot for what,
on which rainy day.
Now it's time to spend
those calories at the gym.

FAT CHICK

I'm really hip,
and tummy,
and thighs,
but terribly wise.

PEAR-SHAPED

Pear-shaped
isn't so very odd
when breasts haven't
fully bloomed.

Turning apple-shaped,
is only natural
as I ground myself
and become symmetrical.

I've often longed,
(like you all)
to be blonde, slender,
straight but tall,

the elusive
banana fare -
curved but not
rounded anywhere.

VERTICALLY CHALLENGED

short and wide,
but, oh, so sweet

queen-size full-measure,
outstretched reach
grasps life's liberal share

wide horizontal smile,
drips sweet volumes
of pungent perfume

expansive, vast
with ample range,
not tall and stately

extensive, compact,
not immense,
chunky, stout, broad

and smells,
oh, so good.

PUTTIN' ON WEIGHT

I've had lots of years
to put on weight:
weight of slights,
hurt feelings, pain,
and disappointment.

I wrapped each cell
with fat to cushion
and protect me:
from you, from myself,
from those
I foolishly trusted.

RIGHT HUNGRY

Grizzly bear roars,
rips berry bushes,
gobbles leaves, stems, fruit,
upturns garbage bins.
Her unbearable hunger developed
from an hibernation season
of birthing and nursing while asleep.

Sorry I snarled at you louder
than my stomach growls.
Right now
I'm right hungry,
hungry as that grizzly bear.

I want to eat all summer,
growl at people without apologies,
legally put on weight, and then
I'd sleep the whole winter away –
without any offspring.

YOU EAT TOO FAST

- to Simon and Garfunkel's 59th Street Bridge song Feeling Groovy

Slow down.
You eat too fast.
You got to make
the cookies last.
Just swilling down
some soda pop
and feeling guilty.

FAT EPITAPH

This wife and mother lies, you know,
where she can fit in her own row.
Not so tall, five-foot standing up.
Much wider than that she was. Yup.
Not very deep, but plenty wide.
There is no room on either side.

LETTING GO

DIETS SCARE ME

I release any excess,
pee, kick off shoes,
strip, remove jewelry.

Then I confront the scale.
Tell me I lost five pounds.
Instead, the digital numbers
scream, "Ten over goal."

Food reduction
probably won't end
in starvation during
my fat-fight training.

But Dad always joked,
his horse "up and died"
just after he finally
trained her not to eat.

NO MORE

Mom said,
"Too much
of a good thing
is still too much."

Dad said,
"Wish in one hand.
Spit in the other.
See which fills up first."

I will let go of want
and focus on need.
Good nutrition
will ensure a leaner body.

But, I do try to deny temptations
of DQ Heath bar Blizzards,
onion rings, sour cream,
even childhood mac and cheese.

No matter what starches
and sugars I desire,
I want excess body fat
no more.

DIET – MOAN

Diet:
salad and grapefruit,
cabbage soup.
No, not yucky carrots.

No potatoes and gravy,
or donuts and cookies,
not even milkshakes
or BBQ chips?
Moan.

It would be
easier to diet,
if I didn't have
any taste buds.

TRUTH ABOUT DIETS

I don't know how
diets end, or when
to cut them off, and why
to start again. It seems
they always begin again.
Until my end, diets perpetuate.

WORD DIET

Lately, I've dieted on words:
sweet, sour,
salty, crispy, crunchy.

Some I've chewed on.
Others have been
hard to swallow.

AU REVOIR

Au revoir chocolait éclair.
Arrivederci lasagna.
Auf Wiedersehn bratwurst.
Adios tortilla.
Sayonara sushi.
Antio yogurt.

My new challenge –
to dine without
sugar, grains,
red meat, dairy,
tomatoes, bell peppers,
vinegar – so many taboos.

I detest invitation avoidance.
Please understand my
reluctance to socialize.
I eat protein, but
from two-legged fowl
or no-legged fish.

I haven't said my final
goodbye to food and friends,
become a total recluse,
or a cannibal . . .
Yet!

FOODS AND TEMPTATIONS

LUAU

What a pig!
Barbequed to perfection
for the Hawaiian party.
Island breezes,
ocean Pacific blue,
hula and fire dancers,
palm trees and
poinsettias,
a December trip
to paradise.

I HATE CARROTS

I despise
nauseous,
orange
mealy-
flavored,
narrow,
crooked
roots.
When
starving,
look for
what is
good.
Carrots?
Scrape,
scrape
off dirt.
Crunch.
Ugh!
No!

FEAST TO FAMINE

Eat, eat, eat.
Stuff turkey, then me.
My "too much" could feed
someone's "too little."
I've lost my appetite.
Send food overseas
with my blessing.

HOW TO LOVE CARROTS

No amount of discussions
about eye sight benefits
enticed me to chew carrots.
Mom said, "If you get
hungry enough you will
eat anything."

She disguised carrots as sweet,
spicy, creamy food.
No matter how smothered,
they were still noticeable.
After she buried them
in spice cake with
cream cheese frosting,
that did the trick.

My adult taste buds
often allow baby carrots
to grace our table.
Grocery list includes
carrot disks for vegetable soup
or shredded salad carrots.

How to love carrots?
When I grew up,
my food options shrank.
When hungry enough,
I learned to . . . like them.

MILK IS FOR COWS

I don't know who decided
cow's milk is for babies.
Mother's milk wasn't for me
or my son either.

His doctor's consultant exclaimed,
"Cow's milk is for cows."
Then his office sent
a hundred-dollar invoice.

Not of the popular opinion,
I thought he was mean.
Maybe he was ahead of his time.
If I had listened

we could have avoided
much dietary distress
and left those cows alone
to feed their own calves.

STUCK ON SWEETS

I'm stuck on honey,
sugar, molasses, and all
the genuine sweet stuff.
Pink, yellow, or blue packets
just won't do for me.

Someday my dentist
may pull that sweet tooth,
when we figure out which
incisor or molar
tempts me the most.

Cravings are intense.
I hope she doesn't expect
to fit me with dentures.

DASTARDLY SUGAR

My social consciousness:
villainous sugar disguises
crumby cookie pushers
as festive friends and family.

Pastries pop up wherever
humans congregate.
Mothers and grandmothers
stir up sticky diet suicide.

Devious plots abound against
my efforts to avoid desserts.
No one intends me harm, but
sugar smiles sweetly at us.

FAIR ENOUGH

I inhaled a funnel cake,
blew powdered sugar dust clouds,

licked a cherry snow cone,
slurped the last sweet juice,

sucked sticky cotton candy
fingers clean,

kicked up sawdust to avoid
tripping on electrical wires.

Scents of hot dogs mixed
in the air with cow manure.

Who wants to hang upside down
swinging dizzy on rides?

Instead I'll overload my tummy
with usually ignored treats.

Campbells ain't got nothin' on
delicate fairground staples.

Mmm, Mmm, good!

ODE TO A POMEGRANATE

We know little of you, oh, ancient fruit,
goddess legend. Oh, tasty thought.
Your odd shape, like a submarine mine,
round, rough, unappealing, explodes with flavor.

While we ponder your healthful characteristics,
wars are waged and starving millions complain.
The cure all, to be all, your seeds squeezed
of their nectar, sucked up as a health potion.

My first whispered love, awakened awareness,
showed me your inner safe. We enjoyed
each seed, one by one, until I traveled
to Hades with Persephone.

Now your life juice is sucked from a bottle
to be part of a gang of the cool group.
You haven't really changed.
Neither has war or love.

I just pity the unfortunate and
kiss a different face.

TEMPTATIONS

Roasted
ears, toasted nuts,
claim this victim once more.
She swallows difficult words like
Diet!

HALLOWEEN SCARE

Halloween candy,
a dietary scare.
See this sweet?
Leftover candy corn
lasts forever.

POPCORN

You microwaved popcorn,
sweetly offered the bowl to me,
but then turned to give it away to another.

Not so bad a deed on the surface,
except your smirk. I knew you –
just being mean and spiteful.

It wasn't the first or only time
you showed me your ignoble side.
You confronted me before I asked.

A fist punctuated your divorce demand.
I sadly agreed, reluctantly at first,
then tasted and enjoyed popcorn singly.

TEMPTED AGAIN

When he's gone,
my habit kicks in.
He dallies on a daily walk;
I search stashes.
He showers;
I frisk the frig.

Alone,
I am dangerous
to no one but myself.

I think,
Don't answer the call
of chocolate turtles
or hidden barbecue chips.

For me, for my health,
I must be diligent
in dietary choices,
whether or not I'm alone.

My friend's advice,
"Stay busy. But stop
writing food poems
when you're hungry."

GRITS IS IT'S

Breakfast? Yummy.
Wake up, tummy.
Look! Bits of grits.

Cornflakes fizzled.
Syrup drizzled,
can't disguise grits.

Poke each taste bud.
Chew like cow cud.
Always it's grits.

Try cheese melted.
When mad Paw unbelted,
I swallowed down grits.

MOONING

I won't waste my time
mooning over moon pies,
manufactured imitation s'mores.

But, over a campfire,
I'd toast one marshmallow
on a straightened
wire coat hanger.

Carefully, I'd slide it onto
a graham cracker.
Gooey and warm, it melts
chocolate bar squares.

I'd squish the cracker cover
onto my s'more sandwich.
Now, that's worth mooning over.

Nope.
I won't moon moon pies.
I haven't the butt for it.

PIZZA, COCONUTS, AND
LAYER CAKE

Perhaps my shape imitates round
and rounded food fare.
Cross off circular foods:
pizza, coconuts, and
chocolate layer cake.

Breakfast: Eggs are – well –
too egg-shaped. So, no round yolks.
Okay, I'll eat the whites.
Bacon strips sit long and thin.
Pancakes are out, but waffles stay in.

Lunch: Neither circular bowl of soup
nor round lettuce, but bumpy cabbages.
Curvaceous apples might
add to my plump waist.
Celery should straighten me out.

Supper: Forget burgers and buns.
Instead, cod swims in butter,
with broccoli florets,
and spinach greens.
Carrot disks are taboo.
Lemon meringue pie
won't top the list.
Chocolate bar must do.

Next week:
Eliminate square foods.

LEFTOVERS

Once, successfully served,
stew, goulash,
or tuna casserole
appeared appetizing
on our family plates.

Another day, attempts
at creative combinations
from lingering leftovers
in our refrigerator's repository
produced food offerings
not reproduced in any recipe book.

Secretly, ungrateful hands,
unceremoniously
scraped inedible entrées
into the garbage pail.

Taken to the landfill,
maybe my meals perpetuated
scavenger birds existence
when they fed on our trash.

Garbage rats survive
without leftovers.
They eat all food when
served the first time.

FOILED AGAIN

This gravy appetite foils inner strength.
My greasy mind re-squeals for tasty breaks.
I think but naught – endure today full length.
These cravings end in snacks and milky shakes:

French fries, Swiss chocolate,
Italian bread, Hungarian Goulash.
Everything ethnic, anything
palatable, is acceptable.

My current biscuit powers weakest will
to motor mushy brain through rampant bites.
My inspiration nets more calories.
This gravy appetite foils inner strength.

TRIPLE DELIGHT TREAT

The triple chocolate fudge,
filled with macadamia nuts,
smelled sooo loud, I became
deaf, but inhaled its perfume.

Insatiable taste buds
arrested my willpower,
demanded one nibble,
a teensy bite, and then
I devoured the evidence.

Calories consumed
in private, overflowed
my favorite blue jeans.
I wiggled and jumped,
but they would not zip.

Thank you, elastic waistband,
my forever best friend.
You stretch and stretch
to let me breathe and bend.

SOCIAL EATING AND DINING OUT

AVOIRDUPOIS DINING

Chic restaurant serves a midget tray.
I swallow salad and attempt to chat,
while coveting much delicious fat.
Daintiness becomes a skill most gray.

I smile at the gracious lipped diplomat.
The plump waiter signals me behind the chap.
I drip lobster butter in the gent's lap,
while trying not to imitate Missus Jack Sprat.

Enjoying the forkfuls, I scooped a scrap.
I view chunks of calorie-loaded pastry,
and indicate to ladle whipped cream vastly.
My husband nudges me with a tap.

He fears my emergent angioplasty.
Gulping, I swallow words overcapacity.

NEVER INSULT THOSE COOKS

Never insult those cooks,
who stir from classic books,
yet boil with attitudes.

Chefs burn with passion.
No fair you dashin'
such tasty bad-itudes!

For sweet saucy fashion,
your gratitude
will gain latitude.

LEERING DATE

Sue's date slurps pasta,
leers at dessert special. . . Her
spaghetti straps flee.

THANKSGIVING 1974

Everyone else finished and left.
He wouldn't, or couldn't, move,
but smiled at the celebration spread,
and sighed and sighed.

Erik sat at the foot of this
six-foot dining table addition.
His two-year-old eyes
catalogued all the dishes:

roasted turkey, mashed potatoes,
cranberry sauce, pumpkin pie.
Whipped cream, smeared on his
chubby cheek, sat out of tongue reach.

Tummy was tightly packed.
His eyes wanted more.
He sighed, took a deep breath,
sighed again and again.

NEIGHBOR'S FENCE

Yellow and purple iris
divide the straight fence line.
One side, pretty flowers.
Their dog barks, patrols,
peeks through wooden slats.

Peek through wooden slats,
see manicured lawn,
clipped hedge topiary.
Invited garden guests
sip rum and laugh.

LADY JANE

"Tea and prune crumpets
taste dusty on prairie soil,"
Lady Jane bemoaned.

MATCHMAKER

He, an experienced Didde Web Pressman,
cannot stop to answer questions.
Deadlines drive him
like a whip lashing a horse.
No time off for playing or romance.
Even business telephone calls
make him cranky. No vacation plans.
He's only interested in the backward
and forward motions of the press. He inhales
the stink of ink messages on rolled paper.

She, an entry-level world-wide-web,
virtual map creator, imagines
traveling places she plans for clients.
Playing on the Internet, her virtual dreams
include a relationship of mutual enjoyment.
Her ethereal thoughts melt like sugar lumps.
Loneliness leads her to consider an ad.
The Mollucan Cockatoo was described
as needing lots of attention,
but it costs fifteen-hundred dollars.

Mutual friend arranges a meeting.

He agrees to Starbucks for black coffee,
only to stop the friend's nagging.
Going Dutch sounds especially fair.
He insists his fifteen-minute break sufficient.

She decides the public meeting place
a pleasant idea. A leisurely cup of latte
sounds delicious. Conversation should be
more interesting than with a needy bird.

Who knows? Sometimes opposites attract.

PASSION FRUIT

Dorothy Parker: The Passionate Freudian to His Love
>   *So come dwell a while on that distant isle*
>   *in the brilliant tropic weather*
>   *where a Freud in need is a Freud indeed,*
>   *we'll always be Jung together.*

He was as passionate as passion fruit,
ripe for self-deception wondering who
talked of him and who didn't. His trips
tripped him up with mother figures.
Engraved invitation stated,
"So come dwell a while on that distant isle."

Where he rendezvoused, no one knew.
He traveled alone on solo flights to rich solitude,
dared not speak of his destination,
to contemplate the latest party favors
            "in the brilliant tropic weather."

He was freed within imprisoning walls,
only his lover's ear tuned to hear.
He feared the shadows whispered secrets
in a sanctimonious sanctuary,
"where a Freud in need is a Freud indeed."

Preparing for the return trip,
he searched the drawers and closets
for love letters he'd squirreled away.
Satisfied they were safe he wrote goodbye as,
         "We'll always be Jung together."

GRATUITY

You plop change
in my outstretched
palm not counting
it back proper.
You're baffled,
when the register
loses electricity.

Slow service,
botched order,
meat arrived cold,
catsup stuck.
Neither a requested
straw nor a water refill
materialized.

You tap your fingers
on the table and
shrug to the next
impatient customer.
I file the receipt,
fold the bills, and
pocket the coins.

For your tip,
I say thank you,
because I think
one of us is
required to do so.

THANKSGIVING WITH JIM CROCE
AND FRIENDS

Operator, could you please
help me place this call?
I want to invite
Roller Derby Queen –
that bleach blonde bomber,
the meanest hunk of woman
down in the arena –
to Thanksgiving dinner.
Speedball Tucker is on a
West Coast turn-around
and will be here soon.

Bad, Bad Leroy Brown
stepped on superman's
cape, when he didn't
heed my warning to not
mess around with Jim.
Maybe we can peacefully
save Time in a Bottle
of Jack Daniels while
the bird roasts in the microwave.

PAPAW'S POSSUM RECIPE

Flumdiddled and penniless,
the Ruritan Society
created a competition carnival.
Busybody neighborhood
davenport gawk-gossipers
encouraged culinary recipes,
formalizing Papaw's
notorious barbequed possum.
Entertainments incorporated
Tennessee's masterpiece
fiddler performances,
silhouetted artisans
of tobaccy-stained embroidery
and welcomed preferential
presentations at tourist gatherings
in Appalachian mountains.
Plentiful toothpicks, but
no possum leftovers.

AWAY FROM HOME IN IRAQ

Freedoms denied, he now defends.
Desert dry thoughts he's pushed away.
With duty and death of close friends,
festive celebrations sit gray.

Camouflage feels dusty, unclean.
Holiday hug memory churns.
Christmastide waves splash red and green
ribbons of hopeful peace returns.

Care package arrives on cool day.
Pictures and fudge shared with bunkmates.
Moods shift to laughter and horse play.
God's blessings from the United States.

HEALTH FOOD

HARVESTING SMILES

You beam
like you won
the Power Ball.
Eyes gleam
with delight.

Your pride
seared
like sunshine
melting snow.
What is it?

I relished your mood.
"Look." You offer
your outstretched
Wal-Mart plastic bag.
I see dirt-crusted cucumbers,

vine-ripened tomatoes,
green peppers, zucchini,
and yellow squash –
your garden harvest,
an all organic inventory.

WHEELING AND DEALING PRODUCE

Officials forced one
Farmer's Market salesman
to admit he didn't harvest
his fare from pristine fields.
Food City produce
produced him a profit margin.
Vegetables sitting
on a folding table
must look more
delicious to customers
in the designated parking lot.

EATING DISORDER

Enjoy your meal.
Don't worry about
starving thousands.

Pay no attention
to outsourced local farmers
or underpaid foreign workers.

Ignore the screams
of slaughtered animals
and castrated calves.

Soy beans aren't
really all that good
for you, are they?

Don't worry about
stinking irrigation ditches.
Enjoy your meal.

Have a cigarette, too.

AVOID A FOOD LECTURE

I traded sugars, starches,
dairy, grains, peppers,
tropical fruits for better health.

With caution I pay attention
to my own body needs. If I pour
high fructose corn syrup into a car,
it won't run smoothly. Neither will I.

Friends and family
ignore my rants to avoid
scrumptious stuff, but
dangerous choices.

I try not to lecture when I watch
them enjoy snacks.
Don't spoil their fun.
Wish I could continue tastier habits.

My own selections
are under my control.
As my tradeoff for sugar abstinence,
I look forward to less sickness.

WHERE ROOT VEGETABLES LIVE

Just beneath the crusted top soil
worms crawl, slugs slither,
rocks solidify and death decomposes.

Many garden plants are visible
spinach, corn, peas, and beans.
All whet our appetites.

We thinned the garden rows,
served teensy carrots and
leafy tops to our hungry rabbits.

They nibbled on the green branches.
Sharp teeth cleanly cut loose baby carrots,
dropped the orange roots to the ground.

Carrots! I knew they were no good.
Even our furry bunnies discarded them.
So much for Bugs Bunny's, "What's up, Doc?"

I JUST NEED

I just need air,
Rob, and Cinnamon
first thing in the morning.
No caffeine or sugar
poison my day.
After my shower
wake up call, everything
fast-forwards to the office,
where I sip my first
tall glass of spring water.

SIMPLY SALAD

You deny art appreciation, and say,
       "The Smithsonian is filled with junk."

Yet, I admire your
       carefully torn, crisp lettuce.

Cucumber slices stand in the bowl's circle.
       Grape tomatoes dot their pattern,

with black olives like red and black
       electrical wires you twist into energy.

I smile at your delightful presentation.
       You frown as

I complicate it –
       add my own cheese, mushrooms, dressing.

I like you growing more creative,
　　　　while teaching me to be less complex.

I'm a bored, struggling artist,
　　　　frustrated and afraid to quit my day job.

You are an electrician lighting museum pieces
　　　　you profess not to appreciate.

We're not a stew, blending each ingredient
　　　　of our individuality,

but a simple symmetry,
　　　　like a salad filled with unique tastes.

DIETARY CHANGE

Burgers and fries,
chips and salsa,
ice cream and cake
dominated.

Fast food frenzy,
quick casseroles,
work break diet,
less nutrition.

Pre-retirement
meatless planning,
vegan thinking
increased my fat.

Now, no soy beans,
dairy, sugar
or grains for bread,
but changed health.

DEEP WITHIN

My inner being wants freedom,
freedom from human decisions
about sustenance and body stretches.
My spirit wants to express itself
deep within this entity's shell.
She only wants me to feed
her existence with meditation
to cleanse and release the past.
She doesn't care to share
with this world, because deeper,
more important considerations exist.
My mind explains human needs,
but my spirit longs to be free,
not stuffed deep within.

AFTER THOUGHTS

I feel we are each a unique human being with different needs. What works for me may not be best for you. Consult your health care professional before you apply any diet or exercise program for your life. I am not a dietician or doctor. I'm only relaying some personal experiences.

One doctor gave me a formula to determine how many calories I should consume for a healthy weight. At the time, I was pretty sedentary. She suggested I use a multiple of 10, because that would be for the metabolism of a slug. Not very complimentary, but I got the idea. She said if I exercise profusely, then I should use a multiple of 15. If moderate exercise is my style, then multiply by 12.

Next I was to calculate how many calories it would take to maintain my current weight. My internal Gemini twin Cassie topped off at 205 so I'll use that as an example. 205 x 10 = 2050 calories. That's how many I needed in order to maintain that weight without exercising. 2050 doesn't sound like much excess, because food label calculations use a standard 2000 calories per day. However, they do not take activity level, height, or bone structure into consideration.

The doctor said if I wanted to lose one pound per week, then I needed to reduce by 500 calories per day which equals 3500 calories for one pound loss in seven days. $2050 - 500 = 1550$ calories per day. If I wanted to eat more, but lose weight, I had to exercise more.

I wanted to weigh 132 pounds. Since I was still pretty inactive, I multiplied by 10 again. So as an inactive person I could only consume 1320 calories per day to maintain that weight. I tried to drop too many calories immediately so I could lose pounds faster. I felt deprived. The diet soon failed.

A nutrition center doctor suggested my current diet, but I tweaked it to include the blood type diet. That resonates for me. Coincidentally, my husband and I are both A positive. That's handy for food planning. This may not be appropriate for others, because of a different blood type or some other reason. My husband's diet doesn't need to be as restrictive as mine.

Currently, my diet eliminates the following. I'm lactose intolerant, so no dairy. Besides breaking out in fat, wheat, other grains, and sugar cause me health problems. I also avoid breads, rice, corn, etc. Tropical fruits contain too much sugar. Stevia is my only sweetener, when necessary.

I allow a small sweet potato or, rarely, a baked white potato every other day. On alternate days, I consume a cup of organic canned pumpkin. Yes, I also eat carrots. I've learned to appreciate them. Speaking of vegetables – on the A+ blood type diet, some are not allowed: like tomatoes, bell peppers, and cabbage. They cause digestion problems. My husband and I note we have less digestive issues when following this diet.

We filter our water and drink 70 ounces daily. As much as possible, we eat only organic foods either raw or gently cooked. According to the A+ blood type, we do best with meat from two-legged or no-legged animals. In other words: fowl and fish. I guess we could also be cannibals. Hmmm. Maybe not.

Cassie and I are finally convinced to add exercise, but don't expect me to ever be an athlete. I do exercise on the Wii most days and I get a kick out of seeing my "fit age" as considerably less than my chronological years. My husband and I enjoy our daily walks in a park, weather permitting. Rob is an athlete who hikes all day long or walks the golf course without a cart. He alternates outdoor activity with the treadmill in a gym. And we are of social security age!

My medical caregiver in a recent Well Lady appointment sent me to another nutritionist. I came armed with a two-week food diary and the sample diet printed on the next pages. The nutritionist said, "If others ate that well, they would be much healthier."

SAMPLE DIET

Breakfast:

2 heaping T of organic blueberries

1 whole organic egg

3 T organic egg whites from a carton

1.5 strips of turkey bacon (non-GMO, no antibiotics, etc.)

Seasoned with Celtic sea salt, parsley, garlic, and onion powder. Cook in a non-stick pan with a spoonful of olive oil.

Lunch:

4 oz of meat (non GMO, no antibiotics, etc.)

Plenty of organic vegetables either in a salad or steamed. Often veggies are leftover from the previous supper.

1 non-tropical fruit, such as an apple, pear, strawberries, grapes, or half a cup of applesauce with cinnamon

I use the same spices as for breakfast, but may add oregano, cumin, or others to add zest.

1 T of ground flax seeds sprinkled on vegetables or stirred into applesauce.

<u>Afternoon Snack</u>: (We call this our beer and nuts.)
1 glass bottle of root beer (stevia sweetened)
1 handful of walnuts or pecans
1.5 oz box of organic raisins

<u>Supper:</u>
4 oz of meat
Plenty of steamed organic vegetables
1 small organic sweet potato OR one cup of organic canned pumpkin. Either one is seasoned with cinnamon.
For dessert we have a 1.5 inch square of unsweetened 100% cacao Ghirardelli chocolate.

As you can see, we don't overeat. Rob adds in yogurt or cottage cheese in the morning. He's not lactose intolerant and needs more generous portions of the other foods since he exercises all day.

Organic foods can be expensive. However, we have fewer illnesses and less doctor visits. Medicine is also expensive. Neither Rob nor I take any prescription drugs or over-the-counter medicines. How many other senior citizens can say that?

It's too bad we have to pay extra for clean food and filter our water. Pure air, pure food, and pure water should be everyone's right. The government should heavily tax the contaminated foods and less nutritious packaged meals. This would encourage people to buy organic foods. After all, poor nutrition contributes to the abundance of expensive health care remedies. Insurance companies should be concerned that their clients are not overweight and charge more when they are. Poor nutrition and excess pounds cause many illnesses. Okay, Polly and I are off the proverbial soap box.

Rob and I avoid dining out as much as possible. When traveling, we reserve a room with a kitchen and shop at the local health food store whenever possible.

Sometimes, I've let Cassie overtake Polly and I would help myself to a sweet treat when out with friends. I try to avoid it, because I usually pay with a health incident or put on weight. I'm not perfect.

My poems were written over the years and you may notice they reflect other dietary choices employed at that time.

I just thought I'd show you my current diet. I'm 63-years-old and currently weigh 132 pounds at a height of five-feet-three inches.

I hope Cassie's temptations didn't make you too hungry. Judgmental Polly can be overbearing at times.

Best wishes for a long and healthy life.

ACKNOWLEDGMENTS

The following poems were previously published in

Pastiche of Poetry, Volume I:
Avoirdupois Dining; Away from Home in Iraq; Diet – Moan; Eating Disorder; Fair Enough; Families; Fat Chick; Fat Epitaph; Foiled Again; Fun Food Thought; Gratuity; Grits is It's; Harvesting Smiles (also published on *All Things Girl e-zine* 2008); I am From; I Hate Carrots; I Just Need; Just a Sliver of Stolen Crumbs; Lady Jane; Leering Date (also published in *Tennessee Voices Anthology 2009-10*); and Matchmaker.

Pastiche of Poetry, Volume II:
Neighbor's Fence; Never Insult Those Cooks (also posted on *Poetic Asides* 2009); Ode to a Pomegranate;   Papaw's   Possum   Recipe (published on *Fanstory.com* 2008 and PST-NE's *Funny You Should Say That* 2011); Passion Fruit; Pear Shaped; Popcorn; Puttin' On Weight; Simply Salad; Squeet and Twirly; Temptations (also   published   on   *Fanstory.com*   2009); Thanksgiving 1974; Triple Delight Treat (published in *Tennessee Voices Anthology 2010-11*,

Lost State Voices III 2010, and PST-NE's *Funny You Should Say That 2011*);Vertically Challenged (also published in *Schrom Hills Park* chapbook 2005); Word Diet; You Eat Too Fast.

Away From Home in Iraq was also previously published in Rose's religiously inspired collection *God, My Greatest Love.*

I thank members of the Poetry Society of Tennessee-Northeast branch (PST-NE) – especially Benjamin Dugger and Marlene Simpson for reviewing many of the poems in this collection.

AUTHOR BIOGRAPHY

Rose Klix was born and reared in Rapid City, South Dakota. She currently enjoys the Appalachian foothills of Northeast Tennessee.

She earned her Bachelor of Arts degree in English with an emphasis on creative writing in 1978 from Dakota Wesleyan University, Mitchell, South Dakota.

After writing poetry for fifty years, she compiled her poetry written from 1962 through 2012 in *Pastiche of Poetry*, a two-volume set.

God, My Greatest Love is a collection of her religiously inspired poetry. This was published in January 2013 by Little Creek Books.

Eat, Diet, Repeat poems represent her food and diet oriented theme. As a life-time weight watcher and healthy eating advocate, Rose knows first-hand how difficult it is to maintain a healthy weight.

Born under the Gemini sign, Rose teases that she always eats for two, but must live in one body. "I prefer Cassie's eating habits, but Polly's size. Too bad, I can't have both."

More author information may be found on Rose's website http://www.RoseKlix.com